LIVES IN CRISIS

Russia
1991–2001

SEAN SHEEHAN

HODDER
Wayland

Copyright © Hodder Wayland 2001

Published in Great Britain in 2001 by
Hodder Wayland, an imprint of Hodder Children's Books.

This book was prepared for Hodder Wayland by Ruth Nason.

Series concept: Alex Woolf
Series design: Carole Binding

Sean Sheehan asserts his right to be identified as author of this work,
in accordance with the Copyright, Designs and Patents Act 1988.

British Library Cataloguing in Publication Data
Sheehan, Sean, 1951-
    Russia 1991-2001. - (Lives in crisis)
    1.Russia (Federation) - Social conditions - 1991 - -
    Juvenile literature 2.Chechnia (Russia) - Social conditions
    - 20th century - Juvenile literature 3. Russia (Federation)
    - Politics and government - 1991 - Juvenile literature
    I.Title
    947'.086

ISBN 0 7502 3432 6

Printed and bound in Italy by G. Canale & C.S.p.A., Turin

Hodder Children's Books
A division of Hodder Headline Limited
338 Euston Road, London NW1 3BH

Cover (left) and page 1
September 1991: happiness
at the end of the old
Communist order: a pulled-
down statue of KGB
founder, Felix Dzershinsky.

Acknowledgements

The Author and Publishers thank the following for their permission to
reproduce photographs: Camera Press: pages 4, 6t, 7, 17, 19, 20, 21, 25b,
26, 32, 38, 40t, 40b, 41b, 46, 49, 51, 53, 55; Popperfoto: cover (left) and
pages 1, 5, 6b, 10, 11, 12t, 15, 23, 25t, 27, 28, 31, 33, 34, 35, 36, 37, 39t,
39b, 41t, 43t, 43b, 45, 47, 48, 50, 52, 56, 57; SCR Photo Library: cover
(right) and pages 3 (N. and J. Wiseman), 8, 9, 12b (Worldpic), 16, 18
(Nicholas A. Spurling), 29 (David Toase), 59 (E. J. Baumeister Jr).

CONTENTS

Mid-1990s: queuing for
potatoes, St Petersburg.

DANGEROUS DAYS

On Monday, 19 August 1991, the world suddenly did not know who controlled the Soviet Union's fearsome arsenal of nuclear weapons. In Russia, people were starting another week of work when news began to be broadcast that power had been seized in a coup and that a national emergency had been declared. Many people heard the news on their morning train and bus journeys. Television channels were not broadcasting but radio stations carried repeated reports that authority now rested with the Emergency Committee and that Soviet leader Mikhail Gorbachev had resigned because of 'ill health'. It was Gorbachev who had had charge of the nuclear briefcase containing the codes for launching nuclear weapons.

All through the summer rumours had been circulating that people within the government, unhappy with the way society and politics were changing, were prepared to seize power. Gorbachev, the political leader of the Soviet Union, was the man behind the sweeping changes affecting the Russian people. He was enjoying a short holiday in the countryside when, in the evening of Sunday, 18, he and his family were captured by coup supporters. When Gorbachev refused to go along with their demands that he support the coup, the nuclear briefcase was confiscated and he was kept a prisoner.

Bus-loads of Soviet troops bar the way to Moscow's Red Square, 19 August 1991. The Kremlin can be seen in the distance.

The coup leaders had the support of some high-ranking officers in the armed forces and tanks were ordered to move down the streets of the capital, Moscow, and take up key positions. Some tanks blocked bridges leading into the centre of the city while others parked threateningly outside the White House, the Russian Parliament building. With guns pointed at the building, the politicians inside seemed at risk of being attacked unless they accepted the coup.

Ordinary people began to gather outside and by midday a small crowd, including journalists and film crews, waited to see what would happen. Boris Yeltsin came out of the White House, wearing a bullet-proof vest under his suit, climbed up on an army tank and denounced the coup as an illegal act. Yeltsin was a politician who stood for the radical reform of Soviet society. He addressed the crowds and said that the coup leaders 'must not be allowed to bring eternal night', and he called on people to reject the Emergency Committee who were spreading 'clouds of terror' over the country.

Outside the White House, Boris Yeltsin rallies his supporters to oppose the coup.

'These monsters!'

'I … went out on my balcony and saw the tanks rumbling down below, on the Mozhaisk Highway. These monsters! They have always thought they could do anything to us! They have thrown out Gorbachev and now they are threatening a government I helped elect. I will ignore the curfew. I'll let a tank roll over me if I have to.' (Regina Bogchova, a Moscovite at the barricades on 20 August, quoted in Remnick, *Lenin's Tomb*)

The White House is protected by barricades erected by opponents of the coup.

Protesters outside the White House lit little campfires at night and huddled in groups around radios. They were encouraged by stories that sections of the Russian army would not support the coup leaders, who were based a short distance away in the USSR government building in the Kremlin. People had been killed by the military, however, and an attack on the White House was feared. A group of women stood at the barricades with a sign: 'Soviet Soldiers: Don't Shoot Your Mothers.'

On 21 August the demonstrators woke to realize that there had been no attack on the White House. It became clear that the coup would not be successful. The tanks turned round and withdrew from the centre of Moscow. Young soldiers, driving

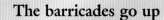

The barricades go up

Baskakov, a retired soldier, took charge of a group of protesters and organized a defence of the White House. He watched as stones and bricks were ripped from the pavements to make barricades to protect the parliament building from the military.

'I used to be critical of the young, but there were bikers, the Rockers, going on reconnaissance missions on their motorcycles across the barricades, giving us news about the troop movements. The young girls that people call prostitutes, they were there giving us food and drink.' (Quoted in Remnick, *Lenin's Tomb*)

Different points of view

'I was there when Yeltsin got up on the tank ... the first day was scary. I was stirred by Yeltsin's words, I wanted to believe in him and to trust him.' (Tatiana, a chemistry teacher)

'Show me one who was running there to defend democracy! Show me! ... Mostly people went there because their friends were going, or they thought they would be in the spotlight of the world's mass . media.' (Nina, an interpreter)
(Quoted in Holdsworth, *Moscow The Beautiful and the Damned*)

Sent in to defend the coup, this tank finished on the other side – daubed with anti-Communist slogans, covered with flowers and bearing the Russian flag.

the tanks away in columns, were smiling and happy, relieved that they had not been ordered to attack. People along the road stopped work to applaud them.

Gorbachev was released and flew back to the capital. He told reporters he was returning to a different country. This was more true than he realized. Yeltsin now called for the disbanding of the Communist Party that had ruled for over 70 years. In the streets, people were toppling statues of public figures associated with the old Soviet system. By resisting the coup, Russians had made a choice to press ahead with radical reforms and there could be no return to the past.

'Worth to stay'

Dr Mikhail Mikhailov considered leaving Russia, but the new mood of reform caused him to rethink:

'When I was thinking to emigrate, some small thing inside me here, it did not accept it fully ... I know only this. This is my country, and somehow I felt it was worth to stay; and I am glad now that I did, because now there is a feeling of, how to say it, like the weather now, of coming spring.' (Quoted in Parker, *Russian Voices*)

THE END OF THE USSR

The dramatic events of August 1991 made up a political revolution that helped shape Russia's history for the next ten years. The events also resulted in the breakup of the USSR and the emergence of new independent states on Russia's borders.

1987: the 70th anniversary of the Great October Socialist Revolution is celebrated in Red Square, Moscow.

The Union of Soviet Socialist Republics, the USSR, had been in existence since 1917. It was ruled by the Communist Party, which took into state ownership the land, industry and commerce of the entire country. The Union consisted of fourteen other states as well as Russia, and Russians made up only about half of the total population. However, Russia's military strength kept the USSR together and no other state had the power to challenge the Union.

By the 1980s cracks had begun to appear in the Soviet system and ordinary people were experiencing its disadvantages. The supply of consumer goods was unreliable and shortages led to queues for goods which were often of poor quality. Russians were becoming more educated and aware that their one-party state should be more responsive to people's needs.

The international power of the USSR rested on its nuclear weapons and military strength. The USA opposed the Soviet system with its own military might and with a different economic system, a capitalist one based on private ownership of land and property. The conflict between the two powers, labelled the Cold War, developed into a competition to see who could spend the most money on technologically advanced weapons systems. The USSR could not keep up with the USA's level of spending and by the mid-1980s the Russian economy was under severe stress.

A Russian joke

Yevgeny Kiselyov worked as a journalist for a state-controlled television station called *Vremya*. He remembers a joke about the days when the Communist Party controlled Russian life:

'A worker, seeing that *Vremya* is screening pictures of Brezhnev [an earlier Soviet leader] delivering one of his long, rambling speeches in his typical slurred way, twiddles with the TV knob, only to find him on every channel. Suddenly he finds a wavelength without a picture of the general secretary and up pops a KGB [government security force] colonel, finger wagging, saying, "What are you doing? Stop doing that!"' (Quoted in Holdsworth, *Moscow The Beautiful and the Damned*)

Gorbachev's problems

In the late 1980s, the USSR leader, Mikhail Gorbachev, introduced a variety of economic and political reforms. He hoped that the Communist Party could steer the country through this difficult period of economic stress. He brought the Cold War to a peaceful end by negotiating with the USA for drastic reductions in nuclear weapons and by withdrawing troops from eastern Europe. Gorbachev did not intervene when countries in eastern Europe abandoned the Communist Party and turned to the West to embrace capitalist systems, but he wanted to prevent the USSR going the same way.

Mikhail Gorbachev visits a factory, 1990. People hoped that his reforms would improve their working conditions and standard of living.

By 1991 it was clear that Gorbachev's economic reforms were not working and people found prices rising and their standard of living falling. His political reforms had also failed. He had removed the Communist Party's dictatorship of power and introduced democratic reforms, but this fuelled the call for

Hard times

Before the attempted coup, Maxim Yallov, a university student, commented on what life was like in the Russian countryside:

'Always the people who are at the top are saying "Tomorrow things will be better, be patient." But it does not happen ... People do not have proper houses, they do not have sanitation or hot water in their homes, they have only poor food which they grow themselves and poor clothes.'
(Quoted in Parker, *Russian Voices*)

Vilnius, Lithuania, 13 January 1991: Soviet tanks move in to take control of the Lithuanian radio and TV stations.

independence from, some of the Soviet states. Within his own party, traditional communists feared that the USSR was in danger of breaking apart and there was pressure to slow down the reforms and reassert the authority of the Communist Party. Gorbachev felt trapped and said, 'I'm doomed to go forward, and only forward. And if I retreat, I myself will perish and the cause will perish too.' The 'cause' was the preservation of the Soviet system but by trying to save it he only managed to destroy it.

1991 began with a violent example of the kind of problems Gorbachev was facing. Lithuania, Latvia and Estonia, three Baltic republics that had been forced into the USSR during the Second World War, had sensed the changed atmosphere under Gorbachev. They began to agitate for complete independence. In January 1991, several civilians in Vilnius, Lithuania's capital, were killed when special Soviet troops stormed the city's television station. Television broadcasts had supported the call for independence and the attack was a clear warning to any groups in the USSR who had thoughts of breaking away. Gorbachev claimed that he had not ordered the attack and worked on new ideas for a reorganized

Ot dushy

Rose Brady visited the Russian town of Naberezhnye Chelny, where the largest truck and engine plant in the world was located, and spoke to a woman trudging along in the snow:

'We began to chat. How did she find the economic situation in the town? "Nichevo", she answered, meaning "nothing special". "I work in the engine factory and they give us food. We get a chicken almost every day". Before we made it to the food store near my hotel, she had reached into her big bag and pulled out a can of herring. "No, no", I protested. "I was only asking about the condition of the town". I didn't need food.
"I am giving it to you ot dushy – from my soul", she replied, holding out the can.'
(Quoted in Brady, *Kapitalizm*)

USSR that would give greater independence to the various states but still keep them within the Soviet system.

In Moscow, Gorbachev faced a challenge to his authority in the form of Boris Yeltsin, a Russian politician who pushed for further reforms and for the democratic election of a president of just Russia (the Russian Federation). Yeltsin had much popular support and in June 1991 he became Russia's first democratically elected president. His vote was boosted by support in the fourteen republics where he supported the people's calls for more freedom.

The end of the USSR

Gorbachev tried to work with Yeltsin and they agreed on plans for a new union to replace the Soviet Union. The three Baltic republics, as well as Georgia, Armenia and Moldavia (which would become Moldova), were not being asked to sign this new treaty. Their claims to national independence were virtually accepted. But Gorbachev still hoped to preserve the Communist Party and maintain a union that at least resembled the USSR. The date chosen for the signing of the treaty was 20 August.

Demonstrators at a 1991 pro-democracy rally hold posters picturing Yeltsin.

Vilnius, Lithuania, 23 August 1991: a statue of Lenin is hoisted down from its plinth, after the new Lithuanian government banned the Communist Party.

This was all too much for the traditional wing of the Communist Party. A letter signed by high-ranking politicians and generals appeared in a newspaper. It declared that 'The Motherland, our country ... is perishing, is being broken up, is being plunged into darkness and oblivion.'

The attempted coup of August 1991 was a last-ditch attempt to stem Gorbachev's tide of reform. At this stage, Gorbachev had little support with the public because he was blamed for the rise in prices, a fall in industrial output and shortages of fuel across the USSR. In July he had unsuccessfully turned to the rich capitalist nations, known as the 'Group of Seven', asking for an urgent loan to stabilize the economy. The failure of the August coup saw a huge leap in Yeltsin's popularity and he was now more powerful than Gorbachev. The very situation that the coup leaders had feared had been brought about because of their failed action.

Events moved swiftly after August and within a month the independence of the Baltic states was recognized. The presidents of Belarus and the Ukraine, two large republics about to leave the Soviet system, met with Yeltsin and signed a treaty to form a new Commonwealth of Independent States (CIS). On 25 December Gorbachev announced his resignation and the USSR ceased to exist.

Away from it all

In 1991 Sergei Molodtsov took a holiday in the remote Siberian village of Oslyanka.

'The people of the village didn't know anything about the political situation. They hadn't heard of Yeltsin, and they didn't know there was a coup. They weren't even interested. No one had any money, but they lived well. They hunted and grew their own food, and there was more than enough to eat.' (Quoted in Handleman, *Comrade Criminal*)

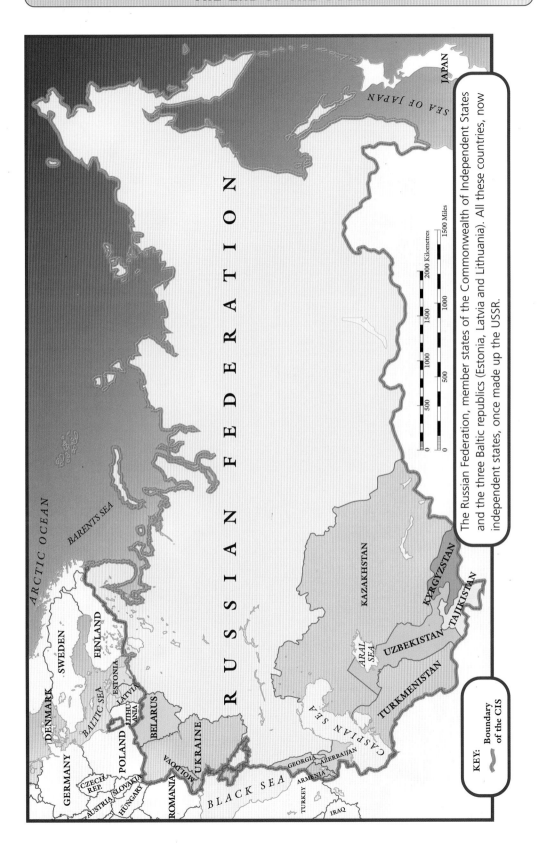

The Russian Federation, member states of the Commonwealth of Independent States and the three Baltic republics (Estonia, Latvia and Lithuania). All these countries, now independent states, once made up the USSR.

KEY: Boundary
        of the CIS

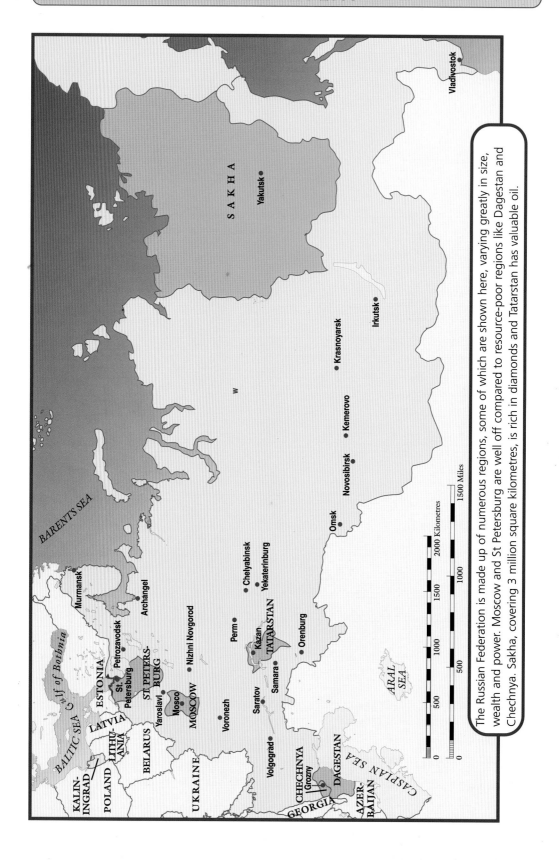

The Russian Federation is made up of numerous regions, some of which are shown here, varying greatly in size, wealth and power. Moscow and St Petersburg are well off compared to resource-poor regions like Dagestan and Chechnya. Sakha, covering 3 million square kilometres, is rich in diamonds and Tatarstan has valuable oil.

SHOCK WITHOUT THERAPY

A complete change

After the breakup of the USSR most Russian people found themselves citizens of the Russian Federation, the largest state in a new Commonwealth of Independent States. Twenty-five million Russians, however, were living in non-Russian states of the former USSR and so became members of ethnic minorities in those states. They could no longer enjoy privileges as ethnic Russians and for some of them the loss of their former status brought problems. In Uzbekistan, for example, Russians in prominent jobs were dismissed from their posts in favour of Uzbek citizens. Those who returned to live in the Russian Federation shared with their fellow Russians the challenge of trying to cope with far-reaching and fundamental changes to their lives.

President Yeltsin visits refugees at a housing project in Moscow, June 1992.

The failure of the August coup not only brought to an end the old Soviet order, but also signalled the beginning of a new social and economic way of life. Changing from the old system to a new one was experienced as a series of crises for most people. In the past, over many decades, Communist Party rule had become accepted, especially after the Second World War when the USSR emerged on the world stage as a nuclear superpower. Living standards had improved and there was a basic but wide-ranging system of social welfare. Prices of everything were fixed by the government. Health care and education were free while housing and energy were provided by the state at extremely low rates. A majority of citizens had

'People did not compete'

Mikhail Friedman was a student during the 1980s. He remembers the old way of life with affection:

'My life was very carefree, just as life was for everyone in the Soviet Union. Materially, of course, people did not live very well, but no one had to worry about anything. The main thing, what was really intense, was friends, spiritual interests, books. The relations between people were far more open. People did not compete. There was not the same disproportion or envy.'
(Quoted in Freeland, *Sale of the Century*)

Workers felt protected under the old system and exercises for good health were organized at the workplace.

believed in the long-term ideals of the Soviet system – socialism through state ownership of property and industry – although they also knew that the economy was inefficient. Gorbachev's attempts to improve the quality of life by tinkering with the system had failed and Russians were now about to experience a radical new approach. Russia was set to adopt *kapitalizm* (capitalism).

Kapitalizm

Changes happened quickly. On the stroke of midnight on the last day of 1991, the fixing of prices was abolished. To soften the blow, the prices of fuel, transport and staple foods remained under government control, but prices for everything else were now subject to demand and supply. This is what is meant by the market economy. People who had carefully put money aside over the years had to draw on their savings to cope with prices rising as a result of inflation by as much as twentyfold in a year. At the start of 1992 a new car could be bought for 10,000 roubles; by the end of the year a

'People are not protected'

Maxim, aged 24, experienced difficulties when his marriage broke up and he left Moscow to work in another part of the country. When he returned in February 1988, he had nowhere to live.

'It's too easy to lose everything in Russia today. People are not protected. Elementary human rights are ignored. Here if you don't have money you have no protection. It couldn't have happened in Soviet times. Then if a person did not work he would be made to work and he could get a propiska [a residency permit] and find somewhere to live'.
(Quoted in Holdsworth, *Moscow The Beautiful and the Damned*)

new spare tyre cost as much as this. It did not take long for people's savings to be completely wiped out and newspapers carried stories of people using roubles for wallpaper and toilet paper, two items in short supply.

Allowing prices to be determined by the free market is only one part of a capitalist economy. Such a system also allows people to buy and sell freely by engaging in retail trade and importing goods from abroad. Under the Soviet system it was a crime, called *spekulatsia* (speculation), to engage in private retail trade, but this law was abolished at the start of 1992. Public markets appeared spontaneously around railway stations, outside food stores and on the pavements of major roads. Many of the traders were senior citizens, trying to supplement their pensions, but there were also housewives, students and working-class people who all shared a need to earn some extra money. At first, anxious to show they were now within the law, they clipped to

Moscow, 1992: sellers and buyers brave the cold and wet, to take advantage of the new free market.

Private owners of kiosks, like this one in Elista in the southwest of Russia, declared their independence by labelling them with English names.

their winter coats a copy of the presidential decree that legalized their existence. In large cities like Moscow, St Petersburg and Vladivostok, glass-and-aluminium kiosks popped up on street corners. Privately owned and sporting names like 'All Night Shop' and 'All for You', they sold a wide variety of imported consumer items including cheeses and ham from Europe and electronics from Asia. In time, some of these traders became more professional and made regular trips to places such as China and Turkey where they could fill their luggage with inexpensive goods to sell at a profit back home. Such traders became known as *chelnoki*, which translates as 'shuttlers'.

Yeltsin's government, backed and advised by economists and financial institutions from the USA and western Europe, now embarked on a more ambitious adoption of capitalism. Yeltsin gained special powers from parliament that allowed him to make new economic laws without a discussion or voting taking place.

Getting permission to trade

Seran Akopyan, aged 45 and the manager of a food store under the Soviet system, decided to set up his own business in 1992. He had the money and he filled in all the forms, but the bureaucrat was reluctant and told him it could take a lot of time ...

'So you tell him you happen to know there is really good beer for sale at such and such a shop ... You ring the shop owner who happens to be a friend of yours, and you tell him to set aside some beer, and of course you tell your friend not to take any money from this bureaucrat but to put it on your account. He goes along with it because he knows someday you could help him. It works perfectly – and you get your approval.'
(Quoted in Handleman, *Comrade Criminal*)

Discovering consumerism

Under the Soviet system, consumer spending was usually restricted to the necessities of life. Vakatova was married to a diplomat. Returning to Russia from Latin America in 1991, she was shocked at the change.

'Russians today consume like crazy. They consume everything new or different. They have longed for this consumerism for such a long time. I didn't consume like this myself, because in Soviet times I had access to the West, to Latin America, but I know my friends could spend everything, just to get this feeling that you can buy something.' (Quoted in Holdsworth, *Moscow The Beautiful and the Damned*)

1992: communist propaganda soon became marketable collectors' items.

Privitizatsia

The single biggest change planned by Yeltsin's economic advisers in 1992 was a programme of *privitizatsia* (privatization). Under the Soviet system, the central government controlled industry and there was no private ownership of factories, shops or industrial plants because everything was under state management. These assets could not simply be put up for sale, because most people could not afford them and Russians would probably not accept small groups of well-off investors brazenly buying up their country's

wealth. Public opinion polls showed that, while a majority favoured the private ownership of apartments and small shops, there was still a lot of support for keeping industry under state ownership. To win public support, the government introduced a voucher system in October whereby every Russian was given a voucher with a face value of 10,000 roubles (worth about £15 at the time). Vouchers could be used to buy shares in companies but they could also be freely bought and sold, as nightly television advertisements explained under the slogan of '*PrivitiZAtsia*'. (*Za* in Russian means to be in favour of something.)

Over 140 million Russians collected their vouchers and, soon after, signs could be seen outside pavement kiosk shops saying *Kuplyu voucher* ('I will buy a voucher'). There was nothing to prevent a wealthy investor or a company, either Russian or foreign, from buying up masses of vouchers and using them to purchase a large stake in a privatized company. This is exactly what happened and it made some people extremely wealthy and very powerful.

Some tempting things were beyond what people could afford.

Raised the wrong way?

Vera Nikiferovna brought up four children on her own after the death of her husband.

'I worked in a sewing factory for forty-one years,' she recalled. 'I started when I was fourteen years old. I got married young, lived with my husband, gave birth to children, raised them, and that's it. I don't have beautiful furniture. I don't have a beautiful apartment. I don't have a dacha or a car. I didn't earn anything in life. Now my children tell me I raised them the wrong way. All that honesty and fairness, no one needs it now. If you are honest you are a fool. They say we are going to live better but I don't know.'.
(Quoted in Brady, *Kapitalizm*)

When will it all end?

In an interview in 1993, one woman expressed dismay that the transition to market capitalism seemed to her to be lasting for ever, without any of the benefits she had been led to expect:

'You wonder when it is all going to end. There's no end in sight at present. No doubt our children will grow up and live out their lives during the period of market transition! We'll still be on our way, crawling there. It doesn't exist, this market transition.'
(Quoted in Bridger, Kay and Pinnick, *No More Heroines*)

Paying the price

As well as the constantly increasing cost of food and consumer items, there was another price that had to be paid by Russians for the rapid transition to capitalism. This price, not one that can be quantified in terms of money, arose from the shock that people felt as their way of living underwent profound change. Other countries in eastern Europe, like Poland for example, had already been through the sudden adoption of capitalism, and the phrase 'shock therapy' was used to describe the experience: people had had to cope with rapid change, but in the expectation that it would improve their quality of life. Such was the speed and pace of Russia's transition that people there began to talk of 'shock without the therapy'.

The transition was especially difficult for older people who had grown up under a different system and become accustomed to it. The security of life-long employment disappeared and workers had to face the crisis of unemployment. Capitalism also brought with it a new set of values, as economic freedom meant that everyone had to look after their own interests.

Even spaghetti went up in price by seven times. As food prices rose, many people started to live on an ill-balanced diet of bread and milk.

Finding a job

A middle-aged woman explained the difficulty of finding employment
in the early 1990s.

'I sometimes look through the advertising papers that they put through
the door … I've only once seen an advert for women up to the age of
forty in all the time I've been reading them. Only once. Usually it's
adverts for young girls to be secretaries, up to the age of thirty, that's
the maximum. It's upsetting, and the main thing, the most unpleasant
thing, is I worry what will happen when I get to retirement age.'
(Quoted in Bridger, Kay and Pinnick, *No More Heroines*)

Money became more important than it ever had been under
the Soviet system. An elderly man told an American journalist,
'We lived for an idea. You Americans live just for money. We
spent our whole lives working for an idea. Now it turns out
you were right.' A Russian woman spoke to the same journalist
about an 'inflation of conscience, happiness, love. With shock
therapy, the value of all these things is falling.' The term
inflation usually refers to the way, over time, people have to
pay more for something. The woman was using the idea to
explain her sense that the worth of personal qualities such as
happiness had become devalued.

No going back

About to leave school to enter the Institute of Foreign Languages, Julia
knew about 'shock without therapy' but did not want the old ways back:

'I think Russia should be a capitalistic country. We shouldn't have the
situation when a stupid, cruel, immoral person should have as much as
an intelligent person. It's not moral. If people behave differently, work
differently, why should they be paid the same?'
(Quoted in Brady, *Kapitalizm*)

During 1992, as the economic reforms began to unroll, there were many demonstrations in large cities. In February, a crowd of over 10,000 citizens gathered outside the Kremlin in Moscow, chanting *Pozor! Pozor?* (Shame! Shame!) and calling for the resignation of the chief government economist, Yegor Gaidar. Other demonstrators, approving of the changes, gathered outside the White House and called for even more economic freedom.

A banner held by pro-communist demonstrators in 1992 pictured former leader Mikhail Gorbachev dressed in Nazi uniform.

Russians also had to adjust to the fact that they were no longer citizens of a mighty superpower. The feeling that their country had lost the Cold War was not a comfortable one and for older citizens this was a psychological blow. After the suffering of the Second World War, when 28 million Russians had died defending their country against Nazism, people had thought that the sacrifice was for the sake of a better future. Now, many people found it difficult to understand what was happening to their country.

'Yankee, go home'

A 48-year-old protester near the Kremlin held a sign saying, 'Da [in favour of] CCCP [the USSR]. Yankee, go home!' She used to teach economics in a school, but now worked as a cleaner. She explained:

'I was not a member of the party, but I believed in the Communist idea ... There are different kinds of Americans. But I am against the Americans who want to come here and influence our policy. I am against the Americans who have an anti-socialist policy. I don't accept the market.'
(Quoted in Brady, *Kapitalizm*)

YELTSIN TAKES OVER

A struggle for power

The failure of the coup in August 1991 was a decisive defeat for the conservative communists who wanted to preserve the USSR. It was not, though, a decisive victory for their opponents who wanted to abandon other aspects of their country's past as well. These people looked to Western countries for their models. They had the support of Western powers, especially the USA, but they did not have a completely free hand within Russia. People wanted change and a better standard of living, but they did not always want a complete break with the past.

Ordinary people had not willed the breakup of the Soviet Union, but they had been unwilling to make further sacrifices to preserve it. Gorbachev had tried to steer a middle way for his country, preserving what was regarded as best about the old system. This attempt had not been successful and Gorbachev lost his credibility with the public. At the same time, many politicians felt that Russia had suffered enough and they wanted to put a brake on further changes. They had support amongst the public but they did not have a dynamic leader. Those who wanted further changes, on the other hand, had Boris Yeltsin as their leader.

We don't exist any more

A former engineer expressed her dismay at the way the new economic order paid no regard to the fate of those who found themselves out of a job:

'And woman like us, all these woman engineers, they were the cream, they were the flower of the nation. They'd been to the most prestigious institutes, worked in the defence industry – they called us engineers but we were specialists in electronics mostly … Now they're all working as cleaners and traders. We don't exist any more, no one is interested in us.'
(Quoted in Bridger, Kay and Pinnick, *No More Heroines*)

Siege of the White House

Yeltsin became a popular politician in Moscow because he championed himself as a people's politician. He attracted publicity by travelling to work on public transport and rejecting the privilege of an official limousine. Unlike many of his opponents, he was able to mix with ordinary people and talk to them in factories and shops. Although he had been a member of the Communist Party, his demand for radical change forced him into becoming independent. He became the leader of the movement for the complete dismantling of the Soviet economic system. His personal bravery in August 1991, when he publicly defied the attempted coup before its defeat was assured, increased his political strength.

The politicians opposed to Yeltsin had their power base in the Congress of People's Deputies, a parliamentary body that had been elected in 1990 under Gorbachev. While Yeltsin claimed authority to rule because he had been elected president in June 1991, the Congress based its power on changes to the Russian constitution that had been made by Gorbachev. Under the constitution, Congress had the right to impeach the president, and a call to dismiss Yeltsin at the end of 1992 almost succeeded. The 1,033 members of Congress voted and Yeltsin survived by only 72 votes. The head-on collision between

Yeltsin talks to veterans of the Second World War, May 1992.

Vice-President Alexander Rutskoi was Yeltsin's rival for power, supported by those who wanted to keep the old Soviet system.

Russians gather to pray for peace, during the events of autumn 1993.

Yeltsin and Congress was played out on the streets as rival demonstrators confronted one another. 'Down with Yeltsin' and 'No Capitalism' read one set of banners while rival placards proclaimed 'Boris, You Are Right'.

Support for Yeltsin

Boris Yeltsin was a hero to some people. A television journalist defended the politician's attack on the White House in October 1993.

'Yeltsin was right to resort to sheer power because he was faced with a rebellion. There were hundreds of armed people full of hatred towards not only the president but everything in the new Russia. They wanted to reinstate [Communist] party rule and end the reforms.'
(Quoted in Holdsworth, *Moscow The Beautiful and the Damned*)

Matters reached a crisis in September 1993 when Yeltsin announced on television that he was suspending the Congress and calling for new elections. Congress, meeting in the White House, retaliated by voting Yeltsin out of office. On 24 September, the telephone, electricity and water supplies to the White House were cut off and police surrounded the building, allowing people to leave but no one to enter.

On 3 October a crowd of people supporting parliament attacked a pro-Yeltsin television station, only to find special police units waiting for them. Government forces opened

Suspicion of Yeltsin

Vasily Filipovich, a 68-year-old retired army officer, witnessed the events of October and concluded that the authorities wanted to provoke trouble so that Yeltsin would have an excuse for attacking the White House:

'Now that I think back to the events of 3 October, I can't help thinking that everything was very well directed. I witnessed many people within this crowd provoking others, acting illegally and trying to make the crowd into an uncontrolled mob.'

His wife, Raisa, added, 'I was ashamed of our government – but they weren't ashamed of themselves.'

(Quoted in Holdsworth, *Moscow The Beautiful and the Damned*)

fire and many scores of protesters were killed. The next day, Yeltsin ordered a tank to fire a shot into the White House where the deputies were besieged. A fire started and within hours the politicians inside had surrendered. The leaders of the opposition to Yeltsin were sent to prison.

4 October 1993: army tanks open fire on the White House.

A setback for Yeltsin

Yeltsin's action did not go down well in Russia. He had acted undemocratically in suspending Congress and provoked a violent confrontation that ended with an armed attack on the country's parliament. Russians were becoming tired of the constant political changes and crises and when elections were held in December 1993 only slightly more than 50 per cent of voters bothered to participate.

Yeltsin, by a tiny majority, won approval in the elections for a new constitution that gave the president sweeping powers. However, the party of the reformers supporting Yeltsin did not win a majority of seats in the new parliament, now called the State Duma, which was reduced in size to 450 deputies. The most votes were won by a nationalist party, and the pro-Yeltsin reformers, who won only 70 seats, were very disappointed. So was the USA – and its vice-president Al Gore, who was in Moscow in the expectation that the reformers would win a clear majority, left early in some embarrassment. On the other hand, Yeltsin had a new constitution that gave the president control over the armed forces and the power to veto the Duma's decisions as well as the power to issue decrees, declare a state of emergency and even suspend the Duma.

Scavenging with the birds at a rubbish tip in St Petersburg, in the mid-1990s.

Points of view

By 1994, many Russians had lost their enthusiasm for politics. Years of economic uncertainty and the constant changes made many people distrustful of politicians and their promises to make life better. The nationalist party that did so well in the December 1993 elections gained popularity because it recognized the broken pride of many Russians. A lot of people felt hurt and humiliated by the downward spiral of events within their country and by the way Russia seemed too willing to embrace Western models of social and economic life. A public opinion poll in 1994 found 54 per cent of people

'The best-case scenario'

While the political battles raged, some Russian women found that their challenge was to deal with old-fashioned attitudes held by men:

'In our society in Russia, men too often use their rights and male privileges, and too often relate disdainfully and arrogantly to the women off whom they're living … The most intelligent, the most sweet man you could find, all the same waits for you to clean his socks. In the best-case scenario, he'll go shopping, and carry the heavy bags.'
(Quoted in Sperling, *Organising Women in Contemporary Russia*)

agreeing, and only 29 per cent disagreeing, that life would be better if Gorbachev had never started changing the system. When asked what they most regretted about the way life used to be, the most common answer was that people used to have confidence in the future.

A street in Nizhni Novgorod, about 300 km east of Moscow.

Making ends meet

Official statistics in 1995 showed that 30 per cent of families were living at or below the poverty line. Even employed people did not always receive their wages regularly, as Olga Samarina explained in March 1995:

'In factories a lot of people simply aren't being paid. My husband hasn't been paid since January. But his 150,000 [roubles] is considered part of the family budget. Although it's not there! … And when the monthly unemployment benefit is 39,000 and the monthly metro pass [in Moscow] costs 60,000 …'
(Quoted in Sperling, *Organising Women in Contemporary Russia*)

A 4 July picnic

One woman, working in Moscow as personnel manager for an American publishing company, came up with a good idea for a holiday:

'Somebody told me how the Americans love the fourth of July holiday. I knew a lot of our employees were complaining about the fact that the company offered them no facilities or recreational activities. So I went to see the management and convinced them to have a fourth of July picnic. For Russians it has no meaning whatsoever but it was a good excuse.' (Quoted in Pilkington, *Gender, Generation & Identity in Contemporary Russia*)

The result of the December elections also affected the relationship between the USA and Russia. The government of US President Clinton had warmly supported Yeltsin and expected the reformers to win popular support for the adoption of a capitalist system. When this failed to happen, another American point of view came to exert more influence. It was argued by some that Russia should be fenced in by eastern Europe and deterred from ever thinking again that it could be a world power. The independent states that had once been part of the USSR should be supported, it was said, along with the countries of eastern Europe, so that Russia would remain weak on the international stage. The result was that during 1994 the USA decided to offer Poland, the Czech Republic and Hungary full membership of NATO (the North Atlantic Treaty Organization).

During the Cold War, it had been NATO armed forces in western Europe that had stood for the West's opposition to the Soviet Union. Extending NATO to the western borders of what had been the USSR, overriding Yeltsin's protest, seemed to be forcing Russia into isolation. At the same time, a carrot was offered in the form of a $1.5 billion loan to Russia early in 1994. If Russia pushed ahead with economic reforms, so many assumed, there would be further loans and agreements.

June 1994: President Yeltsin and Greek Prime Minister Andreas Papandreou exchange papers after signing a partnership agreement between Russia and the EU.

An agreement with the European Union (EU) was also signed, suggesting the possibility of a free trade pact.

While this remained a possible course for the future, it was events within the Russian Federation in 1994 that brought a new situation to crisis level. Chechnya, a state in the south of Russia with non-Russians making up three-quarters of the population, was about to erupt in rebellion.

Window to Paris

In the 1994 Russian film *Window to Paris*, a teacher discovers a magical door in his apartment that leads straight from St Petersburg to Paris. When he takes his class there, he finds that they don't want to return.

'Child: We could work in McDonald's.
Child: We could even wash dishes.
Child: ... or cars.
Child: There are lots of jobs ...
French woman: Come on children, are you not ashamed of yourselves? ...
Teacher: OK, you are right. You were born at the wrong time and you live in a country that is on its knees, but it is still your country. [music] Is it impossible to improve it? So much depends on you, children, believe me. But you don't even want to try? Can you really not care at all?'
(Quoted in Pilkington, *Gender, Generation & Identity in Contemporary Russia*)

WAR IN CHECHNYA

Ethnic separatism

There are 172 different ethnic groups living in the Russian Federation but over 80 per cent of the population is Russian. The Federation has its own sense of identity and calls for independence come only from states where non-Russians make up the majority ethnic group. These states are in the North Caucasus, in the southwest of the Federation, and the only one of them prepared to take up arms against Moscow is Chechnya.

The Chechens are mostly Muslim and they have a long history of struggle against occupation by Russians, one that goes back to the nineteenth century. After the failure of the Moscow coup in August 1991, Chechens seized the opportunity to assert their national identity.

Many Chechens were enthusiastic supporters of the nationalist rebels.

Legacy of the past

Ayub Khansultanov, aged 30, was a Chechen trader before taking up arms to fight the Russians. Aware of past history, he thought that conflict with Moscow would bring another war.

'My grandfather was shot by the Cheka [secret police], Russians who wanted his horse. It was a good horse, he loved it as much as his wife, so they shot him ... We will come at them from all sides, shooting them like partridges. The day may be theirs, but the night is ours.'
(Quoted in Gall and De Waal, *Chechnya*)

Government buildings in Grozny, the state capital, were occupied by armed protesters and, when Yeltsin demanded that they withdraw, Chechens started forming their own army. An election was held in Chechnya in October and although none of the large Russian population voted, the result was a clear victory for the nationalists. The politician elected president of the newly declared independent state was Jokar Dudayev.

Chechnya was in a peculiar state in 1992. The Yeltsin government was too busy changing the economy to turn attention on its rebel republic. In many respects life went on as before. The Chechen soccer team still played in the Russian league and the Russian rouble was still the currency. What was different was a new atmosphere of uncertainty and instability. The crime rate increased rapidly and the large non-Chechen population began to feel insecure. Around 50,000 Russians left in 1992 alone.

Former Red Army general Jokar Dudayev was elected president of Chechnya in 1991.

A black market country

By 1993, although its borders with the rest of Russia remained open, Chechnya was cut off financially from Moscow. No government funds reached the republic and the result was that Chechnya turned into a black market economy. Taxes were not

Cash delivery

When Chechen leaders found themselves cut off from the Russian banking system, they opened a bank account in Turkey. In September 1992 a banker named Imayev withdrew $4 million in cash and returned to Grozny on an ordinary flight:

'I took all the money, four million dollars, in a cardbox box used for household soap. I put two million in each of two boxes. The boxes were dirty and I carelessly kicked them across the floor of the airport. I was rather disreputably dressed as I went through the hall, that's what I agreed with the lads. I arrived back and it saved the situation. One million went on workers in the oil industry, one million went to pensioners, one million went to the budget, one million was kept in reserve.'
(Quoted in Gall and De Waal, *Chechnya*)

Black market prices

The market place in Grozny became like an open-air department store selling upmarket goods, from Japanese electronics to French perfumes, at bargain prices. Gun dealers had their own section and one trader showed a photograph of a pistol with a gold-inlaid handle:

'It's a Mauser [type of gun] we worked on specially. Sorry about the picture quality. The price is 6000 dollars'.
An ordinary Kalashnikov machine gun was only $500.

Khalik, a trader in another section of the market, was selling televisions for $300 that he purchased in the Middle East for $230:
'Some of them are probably not the best quality. Not all our buyers know that of course'.
(Quoted in Gall and De Waal, *Chechnya*)

Invasion: Russian soldiers enter Chechnya, December 1994.

paid by people living in Chechnya and the Chechen government obtained money by selling its oil and becoming involved in illegal arms deals. Chechen criminals formed their own powerful mafia and the republic provided a safe haven for its activities. In 1992, the biggest bank fraud in Russian history was carried out by a Chechen gang who got away with 60 billion roubles ($700 million).

Ordinary people living in Chechnya had to make do as best they could. As many as half the adult population turned to black market trading as a means of making a living. Two flights, filled with traders, left Grozny every day for the Middle East. They returned laden with tax-free consumer goods which were then sold in a large open-air market in the capital. Grozny became the central market for the whole North Caucasus region, the poorest region in the Federation.

By 1994 Chechnya was a lawless state. Yeltsin, who as president was also now the commander in chief of the armed forces, turned his attention to the rebel republic. The December 1993 elections had seen a sudden increase in votes for a nationalist Russian party and Yeltsin hoped to steal some of the nationalists' wind by acting firmly against a state that challenged Russian rule. Russia also wanted control of the valuable oil pipelines that ran through Chechnya.

Invasion

As 1994 drew to a close the battle lines were drawn between Chechnya and Moscow. In December, some 40,000 Russian troops invaded Chechnya; opposing them were only about 1,000 armed men. Western powers, keen supporters of Yeltsin's economic programme, remained largely silent. Plans were made for an assault on Grozny and many thought it would all be over fairly quickly.

A soldier's thoughts

A Russian doctor, an officer in the army that invaded Chechnya in 1994, expressed his doubts about the war:

'We are not doing anything good by being here. We are fighting civilians, it would be better if we left. Almost all the officers think the way I do. It would be senseless to attack Grozny, it would lead to a guerilla war.'
(Quoted in Gall and De Waal, *Chechnya*)

Chechen soldiers leave the capital, Grozny, to take up positions against the advancing Russians.

I have nowhere to go

Tanya Yemelina, a Russian woman living in Grozny, felt she had no choice but to stay in the city and hope to survive the bombardment:

'I have nowhere to go. All I have is my two children, nothing else. Everything I have is here.'

Polina Shakayeva, a Russian senior citizen, said:

'I cannot go. My husband is at home, he is paralysed. I cannot leave him and I cannot move him.'
(Quoted in Gall and De Waal, *Chechnya*)

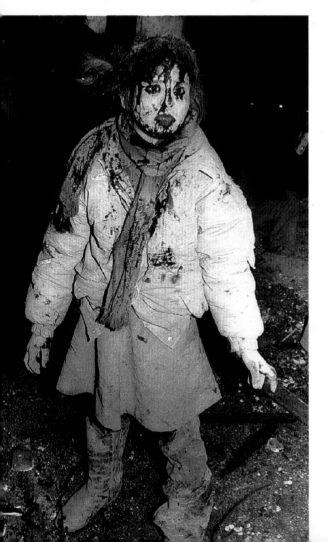

The bombing of Grozny from the air began on 17 December. Families, mostly Russian, moved into the cellars of their homes for protection and on New Year's Eve a bombardment of the city began. A pall of smoke hung over the city, there was no water supply, and tanks advanced towards the city centre where the headquarters of the Chechen resistance were located. Some 100,000 civilians were trapped in the city.

The tanks were attacked by anti-tank grenades fired from the shoulders of Chechen rebels. The tanks were easy targets in the streets of a city their drivers did not know, and where they found it difficult to manoeuvre. One Chechen fighter said a tank in such a situation was a 'moving coffin … One hit is enough.' The Russian soldiers were poorly trained young men in their late teens and they were no match for

January 1995: six people were killed and more wounded when a tank shell exploded at a building where they were taking cover.

their enemy. The Chechens fought with daggers and swords but their lethal weapon was the rocket-propelled grenade that could pierce the body of a tank. This initial attack on Grozny became a slaughter and an estimated 1,000 Russian soldiers eventually died in what was one of their country's most humiliating military blunders.

March 1995: Russian soldiers move cautiously along a street in Grozny.

A lost war

The battle for Grozny began in earnest when the Russians regrouped and planned a new strategy. A massive new bombardment of the city got under way and Russians advanced in small groups, armed with snipers and torching buildings as they worked to flush out the enemy. It took three weeks just to reach the Chechen headquarters and two months to assert control over the city.

The Russian forces were hopelessly organized and for every soldier killed by the Chechens, five died as a result of carelessness and their own mistakes. It was winter and yet gloves were not

New Year's Eve

Alexander Zavyolov was 20 when he was conscripted into the army and sent into Grozny on New Year's Eve in 1994:

'We were constantly firing, at night, afternoon, morning, all the time, throughout the day. Our units went in to take Grozny and were constantly demanding artillery support. Those first days during the storm of Grozny were the worst. No one knew exactly where to fire, where the enemy was, even who the enemy was.'
(Quoted in Gall and De Waal, *Chechnya*)

A Chechen reflects

Gaslan Umarov, a Chechen who fought for Russia in the Second World War, surveyed his burned-out home:

'After fifty years of victory, look what happened to me. They burned my apartment, there is nothing left, not even a spoon … We all lay on the floor, then went down to the bunker. I was in a bunker in 1942 and now again I am living in a bunker. Clinton is coming to celebrate Victory Day holiday and all this is happening.'
(Quoted in Gall and De Waal, *Chechnya*)

Shamil Basayev, the Chechen leader of the attack on the town of Budyonnovsk.

provided and not enough food and water were available to the army. When Grozny was finally captured, 27,000 civilians had died and the city was reduced to ruins. The Russian army was so demoralized that some of its leaders were even selling their weapons to the Chechens.

By April 1995, Russian forces had control over three quarters of Chechnya. Resistance came from villages tucked away in the mountains and the Russians began bombarding them in an attempt to eliminate the rebels. In June a group of under 150 Chechens occupied the southern Russian town of Budyonnovsk, about 100 miles across the border. They seized hostages and marched them into the town's hospital from where they issued their demands. They had over a thousand hostages, and some Russian pilots who were prisoners were executed in order to put pressure on

June 1995: as Russian soldiers fire at the hospital in Budyonnovsk, hostages inside wave white flags and scream at them to stop.

Moscow. An attempt to capture the hospital by Russian soldiers was a disaster and only resulted in killing innocent people. Eventually, a deal was agreed whereby a ceasefire was announced in Chechnya and the kidnappers were given safe passage out of the hospital. One of the released hostages, Tatyana Rybakova, was indignant: 'They shot at us, our own troops shot at us. The Chechens were good to us. They only want Russia to withdraw from Chechnya.'

When the Chechen hostage-takers were allowed to return to Chechnya, they took more than 100 volunteers from the hostages with them, for protection.

A temporary peace

A treaty was signed in July 1995 between the Russians and Chechens, but it did not hold and the fighting resumed. A guerilla war developed as Chechen villages became the focus of armed resistance. In 1996, the year in which Yeltsin was seeking to be re-elected as president, there was a feeling in Moscow that some kind of an agreement had to be reached. In August, over 1,500 Chechen attacked Grozny where 12,000 Russian troops were based. This led to a renewal of talks and a treaty was signed at the end of the month.

Chechens try to get on with 'normal life' amidst the ruins of Grozny, 1996.

A Russian reflects

A Russian mother, who lost her son in the war, gave a journalist her opinion of the war and how she felt at the prospect of her grandchildren being conscripted into the army:

'I don't know what they died for. I have three grandchildren and I've told the military authorities they only go over my dead body.'
(*Newsnight*, BBC, 10 October 2000)

The peace treaty did not solve the problem of Chechnya; it simply said that the question of independence would be put on the shelf for five years. There was a deadline, 31 December 2001, for both sides to reach an agreement on the best relationship between Chechnya and the Russian state. Fighting would break out again before then, so this deadline would never be reached.

The war in Chechnya between 1994 and 1996 cost the lives of 50,000 civilians, 6,000 Russian soldiers and around 2,500 Chechen fighters.

Offices were opened offering information for people trying to trace what had happened to relatives and friends.

OLIGARCHS AND GANGSTERS

Profit and loss

Throughout the years of the war in Chechnya the pace of economic and social change did not slow down in the rest of Russia. By the time the war ended in 1996, private companies had a share in over three-quarters of Russian industry. This is a higher proportion than in some western European states and gives an idea of how rapidly the Russian economy was being transformed. Even two years earlier, at the start of the war in Chechnya, the number of Russian shareholders had already reached half that of the USA's total of 80 million.

The new wealth being produced, however, was not shared equally. There were over 30 million people living on less than $30 a month, while 10 per cent of the population owned half the nation's wealth. 'Everything Marx told us about communism was false. But it turns out that everything he told us about

Haves and have-nots: while some people lived a high life, going out to expensive new night clubs, others – especially pensioners – struggled to make ends meet. In 1997, this man offered his cat for sale, to raise some cash for living expenses.

Looking on the bright side

Vladimir Gusinsky worked in the theatre but gave up his job and went into business to take advantage of the new possibilities.

'I've always had a healthy streak of adventurism in my character and a certain feeling of being bullet-proof. All idiots and madmen probably feel the same way. I always risk everything. A man must regularly, every five to seven years, change his life. If he doesn't do that ... girls stop loving him, and his own children stop respecting him.'
(Quoted in Freeland, *Sale of the Century*)

capitalism was true.' This remark was made to the author of a book called the *Sale of the Century*, about Russia's transition to a free market economy, and it sums up how many people felt about what was happening to the country. Marx was a political thinker of the nineteenth century who argued that capitalism was deeply flawed and that communism would be better. Russian people knew from their own experience that the kind of communism practised by the USSR could not deliver consumer goods as successfully as a capitalist economy. They were also now beginning to feel the truth of Marx's criticism of capitalism, that it was unfair and made people unhappy.

Looking on the dark side

Twenty-three year-old Valery, living in a small Russian village, saw his place in a continuing history:

'Our great-great-grandparents were the tsar's serfs, our grandparents and parents were the Politburo's serfs and we are Yeltsin's bums. We are too poor to leave, and there's nothing to do for us here if we stay. We just drink, go wild, and steal our neighbour's chickens. What is the point of working – every day just gets worse and worse.'
(Quoted in Freeland, *Sale of the Century*)

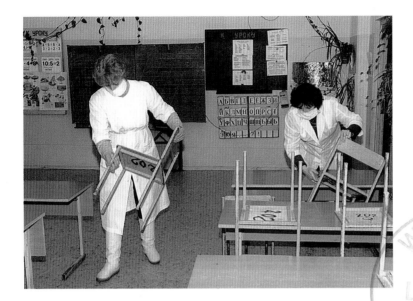

January 1997: medical workers disinfect a school after 35 pupils were taken to hospital with diphtheria – once a rare illness, which returned to Russia as standards of health care declined.

An unhealthy society

Under the old Soviet regime there had been a comprehensive health care system organized by the state. Every citizen had been entitled to free medical care. Under Yeltsin there was no longer enough money to maintain this health service and people had to start paying for services and medicines. This, alongside a general drop in family income, resulted in a serious decline in people's health. Epidemics of measles and cholera returned to the country, partly because of poor public hygiene and partly because people could no longer afford immunization. People were urged to boil drinking water because there was not enough money to maintain a clean supply. Children's health has also suffered because many families could not afford school meals. By the mid-1990s, life expectancy for adult males fell to 58, a figure matched only in Third World countries in sub-Saharan Africa.

St Petersburg, 1997: Russian militiamen carry away a drunken street cleaner who fell asleep and was at risk of death in the extreme cold.

Alcoholism, a cause of early death through heart disease and other ailments, has also reached alarming levels in Russia. By 1996 it was estimated that the average Russian was drinking up to five bottles of vodka a week. The number of people who died from accidental alcoholic poisoning was 100 times higher in Russia than the USA. Yeltsin himself was widely reported to suffer from a drink problem and news stories featured accounts of the president in embarrassing situations. At one international event where a military band was playing, Yeltsin took the baton of the conductor and tried to conduct the orchestra himself.

Getting re-elected

The most profitable sectors of the Russian economy had not been privatized in the first sell-offs that got underway in the early 1990s. By 1995, one year before Yeltsin hoped to get re-elected as president, the decision was made to privatize half a dozen of the biggest and most valuable economic enterprises in Russia. These included the tremendously profitable oil industry and other concerns where the government had enjoyed a monopoly.

Unlike the first wave of privatization, the new sell-offs would not involve vouchers and the general public. Instead, a small group of influential and rich businesses offered a substantial loan to the government in return for control of the new industries about to be privatized. It was also understood that the banks and businesses would support Yeltsin in the presidential election. Indeed, it was planned that only after the elections would the businessmen get real control of the privatized industries. Ulyukaev, a government economist, explained the deal by saying, 'We gave them just one of two keys [to ownership of the industries]. They would receive the second key only after the elections.'

Business people were worried because Yeltsin had not only lost a lot of popular support but was losing it to a new communist party. The new

The big sell-off

Looking back over the years of change, Emma Gushina came to a dismal conclusion:

'I'm no economist, but for me one of the most painful things has been the way our natural resources have been sold off and wasted. But probably Yeltsin is not to blame alone; no person can save a sinking ship on his own.'
(Quoted in Holdsworth, *Moscow The Beautiful and the Damned*)

Watching an election

Curiosity led two students, Marina and Andrei, to attend an election meeting in 1996 where the speaker was Zyuganov, the leader of the new communist party.

Marina: 'We've just come to see Zyuganov, to see what a communist leader actually looks like.'

Andrei: 'When our moms and dads were young, they used to say the sort of things Zyuganov is saying now.'

Marina: 'We will probably end up voting for Yeltsin not because we like him, but because we like reforms. He is the lesser evil.'

(Quoted in Freeland, *Sale of the Century*)

communist party drew support from people who had become disillusioned with life in the new Russia. If the communist candidate beat Yeltsin in the election for president, this would put a brake on the privatization programme. As a result, money was poured into the presidential campaign on behalf of Yeltsin. Even more importantly, all the television stations and the main national newspapers vigorously supported Yeltsin and denounced the communists. One television advertisement showed images of people scavenging for bits of food from the period after 1917 when parts of the country were engulfed in civil war. The message 'Save, preserve Russia. Don't vote for the Red Colour [communism]' appeared on the screen, suggesting that a vote against Yeltsin meant a return to communist dictatorship and shortages of food.

Gennady Zyuganov was the communist candidate who so nearly defeated Yeltsin in the elections of 1996.

Yeltsin had been behind in public opinion polls and was also in poor health. With the help of the mass media, however, he pulled ahead of the communists and just won the election in

Voting for Yeltsin

One elderly woman had no doubts who she would vote for in the 1996 election:

'All my youth, I suffered from the Communists. They told me what to wear, what to eat, what to sing. We should never have that again. Yeltsin has made mistakes. But you have to think of the future, of the lives of our children and grandchildren. All the pensioners in my building are for Yeltsin.'
(Quoted in Brady, *Kapitalizm*)

Voting for the Communists

Yuri voted for the new communist party, which he called by the old name of Bolsheviks:

'I voted for the Bolsheviks, of course. I don't think life will be better, but we didn't have such a collapse of the economy before. Our children didn't wash cars. There was guaranteed education ... The country has become unpredictable. If before we had a guaranteed wage, now it's a different situation.'
(Quoted in Brady, *Kapitalizm*)

July 1996 with a little over 50 per cent of the vote. In September, Yeltsin admitted that he was seriously ill and that he had suffered a heart attack during the election.

Oligarchs and gangsters

After the election, it was pay-back time. The bankers and business people who had supported the Yeltsin campaign were now able to reap their rewards. Vladimir Potanin, who had founded Russia's largest private bank, was able to acquire ownership of a state enterprise that produced 20 per cent of the world's supply of nickel and 40 per cent of its platinum. It cost only $130 million, a very small amount for such a valuable company, and deals like this made up what was called the sale of the century.

Businessmen like Potanin became known as the oligarchs, a word for a small number of people who control a government. It was no surprise when Potanin became deputy prime minister. Another one of the

oligarchs gave an interview to a Western business newspaper and claimed that seven top bankers controlled half of Russia's economy and had a decisive say in political decisions. This did not worry the world of business. The stock market rose and foreign investment increased for the first time in over two years. At the same time, the government was short of money and many people were not receiving their wages.

Russia had become a free-for-all society where rich people could become extremely rich and where gangsters were tempted to take advantage of the situation. Powerful criminals, members of Russia's *mafiya* (mafia), began to exert their influence on people's lives. There was a dramatic rise in the crime rate and the police were underfunded and increasingly corrupt. To test the situation, a truck carrying vodka was sent across the country in 1995: it was stopped by the police 24 times and on 22 of these occasions a bribe was asked for. Many people had lost faith in the government and, feeling unprotected, were

Banker and businessman Vladimir Potanin became one of two deputy prime ministers in 1995.

Changing values

Tatiana, a junior school teacher in Moscow, saw how life had changed:

'In Communist times people were not allowed to do anything or have anything. Right now there is the chance to earn heaps of money and people cannot conquer their urge and cannot realise what is most important in life and what is not. Very often people believe that the more they have, the better. There have always been such people in Russia, it's just that right now they are blooming and flourishing.' (Quoted in Holdsworth, *Moscow The Beautiful and the Damned*)

A gangster speaks

Viktor spoke about his work for the mafiya as if it were an ordinary job.

'A person comes home. We put a plastic bag on his head. We hold it there for a long time. We beat the person, or hold the plastic bag – and there, the person signs all the documents. That's all there is to it. There are a lot of murders connected to real estate – alcoholics, old people.'
(Quoted in Brady, *Kapitalizm*)

A young private security guard displays her skills at a presentation in 1995.

prepared to pay the mafiya. By 1997, around 75 per cent of all businesses in large cities were thought to be paying protection money to the mafiya. As a popular joke put it, 'the mafiya is like a government – except that it works'. Such was the lack of faith in the police that over a million people were employed as private security guards. The kind of large company that was sold off after the 1996 election might employ as many as 20,000 guards, many of them heavily armed. It was not

uncommon for individual businessmen to be shot down in the street, murdered by gangsters whom they had crossed in a deal.

Another crisis

By 1997, Russia was in trouble on most fronts. Yeltsin had won the election but the country was still divided over the best way forward. The economy had been privatized but the government did not have enough money to pay wages, living standards were declining, and a lot of the profits that were being made were ending up in banks outside of Russia. In March 1998, Yeltsin sacked his entire government and formed a new one. It was, as a Western observer said, 'good theatre but poor politics'.

Another major emergency came in August 1998 when Russia fell victim to a global financial crisis that had originated in Thailand in Asia. The Russian rouble fell to less than a third of

By 1998 food queues had returned to the streets of Moscow.

'Worthless paper'

Sasha, a Moscow shopkeeper, explained how she experienced the financial crisis in 1998:

'We work with an American businessman, he supplies us with goods, inexpensive but good-quality Taiwanese clothing. All summer long we sold them well and paid our supplier in roubles. But yesterday when we brought him the roubles he said, "Why have you brought me sheets of worthless paper? The market is frozen, I can't sell roubles for dollars."

So now, he won't sell us the goods any more. And we understand him. He just sits in his office all day long and reads the newspapers and cries.'

(Quoted in Freeland, *Sale of the Century*)

Not the Third World, but in September 1998 charities were distributing food to needy citizens in Russia.

its value before the crisis and people rushed to change what they had into dollars. Incomes fell by 75 per cent and everywhere people lost their jobs or had their wages cut. Many banks closed their doors because they were near to bankruptcy. In February 1999 one bank was robbed by a retired army officer. He did not regard himself as a thief and demanded only the return of his life savings which he had deposited in the bank.

'Absolutely different'

Andrei Pedorenko, working in a financial institution, had a difficult decision to take concerning three people working under him.

'These were good people, members of staff without whom I was going to have problems in my department. But I had to fire them and do it there and then ... I had to make a choice. The difference was so little between those who were fired and those who stayed, it was virtually by chance I made the decision. I didn't have a heart attack when I told them, but I felt very close to it. It's clear to me that we are gradually moving to a world absolutely different from that which we were brought up in.' (Quoted in Holdsworth, *Moscow The Beautiful and the Damned*)

A NEW RUSSIA?

The Yeltsin years

Boris Yeltsin was at the centre of Russian history throughout the 1990s, but not everyone agrees about the value of his achievements. Some people praise him as the man who led the movement towards democracy and a market economy that will bring Russia into line with most of the rest of the world. Critics point to Yeltsin's undemocratic measures, like his attack on the White House in 1993 and his decision to launch a war against Chechnya in 1994. Critics also argue that under Yeltsin Russia's economy staggered from one crisis to another and that the privatization programme was unfair and disastrous for many citizens. Another charge is that Yeltsin and his supporters pushed Russia into a state of debt and dependence on Western financial institutions. Many supporters of the communists who challenged Yeltsin believe that Russia, a once great international power, has been humiliated by the West.

It is true that the Russian economy remains in a precarious state of health. It has shrunk to just a little over half its size in some ten years, something that did not even happen in the Second World War when the country was invaded by Nazi Germany. Russia, the once-feared nuclear superpower, now

By 1998 anti-Yeltsin demonstrations were common in Russian cities.

The cost of corruption

Oleg worked as a driver for a large telephone taxi service in Moscow:

'Our firm has about 600 drivers on its books ... Until the crisis [the financial crisis in 1988] the firm was paying about $6000 a month [in protection money]. It's all very normal. We pay the money; they look after us. That's how things work in Russia.'
(Quoted in Holdsworth, *Moscow The Beautiful and the Damned*)

31 December 1999: President Yeltsin announces his resignation in a TV broadcast.

produces less than Belgium and not a great deal more than neighbouring Poland. Corruption continues to be a fact of daily life. Moreover, it is not only the economy that is in poor health, as the increasing number of citizens dying from the consumption of counterfeit vodka indicates. At the beginning of 2000, the tax on vodka was increased by 40 per cent and this led to an increase in the distribution of cheap, illegal vodka. Some of this black market vodka is not properly distilled and includes lethal methyl spirits. In the first half of 2000, some 21,000 Russians died from drinking toxic liquor and this figure was almost half as many again as the number who died in the same period of 1999.

What happened to Yeltsin?

Yeltsin had proved a surprise winner in the 1996 presidential elections but he was not going to be a contender in the next elections in 2000. After the financial crisis in 1998, hundreds of thousands of Russians across the country took part in protests calling for his resignation. In one television poll conducted in October only 1 per cent approved of his presidency. Yeltsin's state of health continued to deteriorate and he shocked the country by appointing five new prime ministers in the space of just seventeen months. Stories and rumours of his high-handed manner of dealing with people were common.

In August 1999, the obscure Vladimir Putin was chosen as Russia's new prime minister. On the eve of the third millennium, 31 December, Yeltsin unexpectedly resigned in favour of Putin. In the presidential elections in March 2000, Putin won by a landslide.

Man overboard

Alexander Korzhakov, Yeltsin's bodyguard, remembers an incident on a river boat when his boss became annoyed with his press secretary, Vyacheslav Kostikov. The bodyguard was on the deck below and caught the conversation:

"'Vyacheslav, take off your shoes. They're expensive Italian ones, you'll wreck them.'
"It's fine, don't try and frighten me," parried our comedian.
"Throw him," the President ordered and they calmly tossed him overboard ...
Suddenly Kostikov flew past me, his arms and legs jerking desperately. At first I took him for an enormous bird, but an instant later I recognised the familiar bald head and dashed up to the third deck.'
(Quoted in the *London Review of Books*, 2 April 1998)

There remains some mystery as to why Yeltsin resigned so hurriedly and rumours abound. Since the event he appeared in public on only a few occasions, looking unhealthy and bloated. Rumours circulated in Russia that he had bought a house in western Europe in case he had to leave the country for fear of being convicted on criminal charges.

When Vladimir Putin was inaugurated as president in 2000, most Russians knew very little about him.

'I am living'

Having experienced the years of turmoil and change, Serafima Ivanovna felt she had been lucky:

'I am living ... I'm not starving. I can't complain ... I worked in the steel kombinat thirty years. And before that I was head of a kindergarten and a *dom otdikha* – resort. I have three children – and not one of them is an alcoholic. There's not a hooligan among them.'
(Quoted in Holdsworth, *Moscow The Beautiful and the Damned*)

Vladimir Putin

It would have been difficult to predict that Vladimir Putin would become the next president of Russia. He had been a colonel in the KGB, the secret security force during the Soviet era, and was not well known to the Russian public. Perhaps this was a factor in his favour because he was not closely associated with Yeltsin and his reformers and could not be blamed for things that had gone wrong. A public opinion poll in the summer of 2000 showed Putin's popularity soaring to 70 per cent among the public.

Part of the reason for the new president's popularity was the sense among Russian people that Putin represented a break with the Yeltsin era. Under Yeltsin, some of the governors of Russia's 89 regions were powerful figures who could defy Moscow and operate independently of the central government. Putin appointed seven 'super-governors' to re-impose the government's authority. He was also seen to challenge the power of the oligarchs and insist on the right of the government, based at the Kremlin in Moscow, to direct Russia's affairs.

Living with crises

Andrei Pedorenko, aged 36, tried to be philosophical about the non-stop pace of change:

'It's well known that human beings experience crises from time to time. In life you have your white and your black periods and these are always changing ... If in the past you could say that you had lived for a couple of years without any major problems, today it is impossible to say that.'
(Quoted in Holdsworth, *Moscow The Beautiful and the Damned*)

In August 1999 a bomb exploded in Moscow in an underground shopping mall opposite the Kremlin, killing one person and injuring 40. Over the next two weeks a series of bombs exploded in the capital and southern Russia, killing some 300 people. The country went into a state of panic and the finger was pointed at Chechen rebels. In September, Russian warplanes bombed Grozny and unleashed a second war against Chechnya. This decisive action won the support of the public and helped establish Putin's popularity. In August 2000, another bomb exploded in the heart of Moscow and killed seven people. Once again people blamed the Chechen rebels, although no claims of responsibility were made for any of these bomb attacks. The war in Chechnya still goes on.

September 1999: an eight-storey apartment building in Moscow was destroyed by a bomb explosion.

The support for Putin's firm intervention in Chechnya came from people who had watched their country gradually decline in importance. By taking decisive action, Putin presented himself as a decisive leader who would take action to restore Russia's self-respect. Events in August 2000 concerning a nuclear submarine, the *Kursk*, proved to be a setback for Putin's reputation.

The *Kursk* nuclear submarine was regarded with pride.

The *Kursk* tragedy .

On 12 August 2000 an explosion occurred underwater on the Russian nuclear submarine, the *Kursk*, and 118 members of the crew were trapped over 100 metres below the Barents Sea. It was not known if any of them had survived the explosion. The Russian navy's attempts to mount a rescue operation were plagued with delays and inefficiency, and it took seven days before they admitted to difficulties. It required Norwegian and British specialist equipment and divers, whose offers of help were first refused, to get the outer hatch open and confirm that the submarine was flooded and that no one had survived. The cause of the explosion has still not been explained.

The *Kursk* disaster and the poor response of the government provoked much criticism in Russia. For the first time since being elected, Putin came in for blame, and the fate of the submarine was seen as an example of Russia's problems. The *Kursk* had been regarded as one of the country's top submarines and cost one billion dollars; the salary of the captain was $250 a month. In a letter to one of his crew, the captain described the *Kursk* as 'one of the most modern, battle-capable vessels not only of Russia but of the whole world'. This

What if a country betrays its people?

The son of Mrs Valentina Avelene, a builder, was serving on the *Kursk* at the time of the accident. She had advised him to evade the compulsory call-up for military service that came in the autumn of 1999 but he had wanted to serve his country. She said:

'I'd like to see Putin put in a boat and sent to the bottom of the sea – to experience what they went through. People get punished when they betray their country. But what if a country betrays its people?'
(Quoted in *The Guardian*, 21 August 2000)

Last words from a lost son

Mrs Avelene received a letter from her son, Seryozha, on the day that the *Kursk* went down. Seryozha was the lowest ranking member of the crew and had just been promoted to the rank of cook. He wrote:

'Congratulations on passing your driving test. So can you really drive a car now? To be honest, Mama, I cannot imagine you at the driving seat ...We were baptised as submariners – we were called to the command post where everybody drank a cup of sea water and kissed a greased ship's hammer – and then we got these papers and the commander shook everybody's hands. But after drinking the sea water, we all felt a bit sick ... Well, I have probably already begun to bore you with my letter, so I'll stop. Bye, I love you. I kiss you. Write to me.
Seryozha (a cook)'
(Quoted in *The Guardian*, 21 August 2000)

letter, written from the *Kursk*, was hand-written on cheap, rough brown paper and it seemed alarming that the captain of one of Russia's most advanced submarines had no access to a typewriter, let alone a computer. The navy did not release the identities of those who died and when a national newspaper published their names and ranks it declared that it had had to bribe navy officers with £400 to obtain the list.

The submarine sank off the coast of Murmansk in northern Russia and immediately after the disaster the parents of crew members were anxious to travel there so as to be close to the rescue operation. The government did not provide any assistance and desperate parents were left to themselves to wonder what was happening and cope with their trauma.

Relatives of *Kursk* crew members boycotted a national day of mourning and held their own ceremony for the dead, above the site of the submarine.

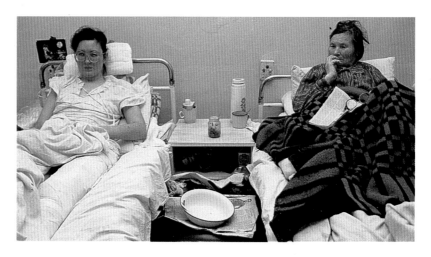

These patients at a hospital in Kaliningrad in 1998 would have received better treatment under the old communist system.

A Third World state with snow?

Ten years after the momentous events of 1991, the future of Russia remained uncertain. In some respects the prospects in 2001 were bleak. For all its problems, the old Soviet system had provided its citizens with a functioning social system and a health service. The new Russia that had emerged during the 1990s had experienced so many crises – social, economic and political – that the strain was beginning to tell. Russia's population was falling by 1,000 a day as deaths exceeded births by almost two to one. Life expectancy for a male was still below 60, for a woman 72. The new Russia at times seemed to resemble a Third World country. Boris Kargalitsky, a politician who was arrested for his anti-Yeltsin opinions, feared that Russia would become 'a Third World state with snow'.

Something to regret

A translator and interpreter, Nina looked towards the future but with regrets about what had been lost:

'It would be very sad if in the next five or six years people failed to find some kind of idea, whether it is the reunification of Russia, the restitution of the Soviet Union or just some cultural concepts. Call it what you want, people need something to organise around, not just wages, prices, the cost of living. Kids should be given something to dream about, not just fat wallets or luxury cars. There should be some centre to life.'
(Quoted in Holdsworth, *Moscow The Beautiful and the Damned*)

Happiness and money

Tanya, a 26 year-old housewife in Moscow, looked back over the years since 1991:

'I have a lot of freedom, but it frightens me. Sometimes I don't know what to do with my freedom. I'm even frightened to have too much money, as too much money in today's Russia simply brings too many problems. In my life before that moment in August 1991 when everything changed, we never said that our happiness depended on the sum of money we had; our happiness depended on everything.'
(Quoted in Holdsworth, *Moscow The Beautiful and the Damned*)

At the old Park of Socialist Progress, Moscow, August 2000. What would the next decade hold?

There were also reasons for thinking that Boris Kargalitsky would be proved wrong. Some good aspects of the way of life under the old Soviet system still survived. Street crime (not counting mafiya crimes) remained rare and traditional rules of behaviour on public transport still applied. Single women could travel home late at night without fearing for their safety. Russia, occupying half of the northern hemisphere, was still the biggest country in the world and possessed the second biggest nuclear arsenal. The Commonwealth of Independent States, formed in 1991, may in the future develop into a regional power. The Russian Federation remained a great country, with over 140 million people, stretching from Norway to China. It would always be a country with a lot of snow, but it may well emerge from its decade of crises as a strong and healthy nation.

DATE LIST

1917

October — Russian revolution overthrows tsarism and leads to creation of the Union of Soviet Socialist Republics (USSR) under the control of the Communist Party.

1985

11 March — Mikhail Gorbachev becomes leader of the Soviet Communist Party. He sets about major political and economic reforms.

1989

12 September — A pro-Western government takes power in Poland.

6 December — Communist rule is ended in East Germany.

1991

13 January — Soviet forces attack demonstrators in Lithuania and 15 people are killed.

12 June — Boris Yeltsin is elected president of Russia.

19 August — Attempted coup in Moscow. Gorbachev arrested but Yeltsin defies the coup leaders and calls for resistance.

21 August — Tanks withdraw from Moscow. Gorbachev is released. The coup has failed.

7 September — The Baltic states of Lithuania, Latvia and Estonia are recognized as independent.

8 December — Presidents of Belarus, Ukraine and Russia sign a treaty to abolish the USSR and form the Commonwealth of Independent States (CIS).

31 December — Gorbachev resigns and the USSR ceases to exist.

1992

1 January — Prices, fixed under Soviet system, are freed. Prices sky-rocket. The legalizing of private retail trade follows.

15 February — Anti-market demonstrators protest outside the Kremlin at the unfolding economic reforms.

1 October — Privatization gets under way with introduction of voucher scheme.

1993

20 September — Yeltsin, acting unconstitutionally, suspends the Congress of People's Deputies.

24 September — The White House, home to the Congress, is blockaded by police.

3 October — Anti-Yeltsin demonstrators attack a television station in Moscow and scores of protesters are killed by government forces.

4 October — Yeltsin orders a tank to open fire on the White House. Those inside surrender.

12 December — Yeltsin supporters gain a tiny majority in elections. A new constitution, giving more power to the president, is enacted.

1994

12 December — Russian troops invade Chechnya.

17 December — Grozny, capital of Chechnya, is bombed from the air.

31 December — Russian troops and tanks attempt to capture Grozny but meet stiff resistance.

1995

15 April — Russian forces control three-quarters of Chechnya.

14 June — Chechen rebels take hostages in Budyonnovsk.

1996

3 July	Yeltsin, surprisingly, defeats Zyuganov (communist canddate) in election for president.
5 August	Chechen rebels take Grozny.
23 August	Chechens sign an agreement that brings hostilities to an end.
5 November	Yeltsin undergoes heart surgery.

1997

21 March	Yeltsin and Clinton meet in Helsinki to discuss expansion of NATO.

1998

17 August	Russian financial crisis. The rouble is devalued, share prices plunge.
23 August	Yeltsin sacks his entire government and forms a new one.

1999

12 May	Yeltsin sacks his government again.
16 August	Vladimir Putin becomes the new prime minister.
9 September	A bomb destroys a Moscow building and kills 94 people. Part of a series of bomb attacks blamed on Chechens.
23 September	Russian warplanes bomb Grozny, marking the start of a second war in Chechnya.
31 December	Yeltsin resigns as president in favour of Putin.

2000

26 March	Putin wins new presidential elections by a landslide.
8 August	Bomb blast in Moscow kills 7 people, blamed on Chechens.
12 August	Explosion on nuclear submarine, the *Kursk*, in the Barents Sea.

RESOURCES

RECOMMENDED READING

Chrystia Freeland, *Sale of the Century*, Little, Brown and Company, 2000. (A Canadian journalist, living in Russia between 1995 and 1998, interviews people affected by the economic reforms of 1996.)

Carlotta Gall and Thomas De Waal, *Chechnya*, Pan, 1997. (Eyewitness accounts of events in Chechnya from the Russian invasion at the end of 1994 to the short-lived treaty signed in 1996.)

Nick Holdsworth, *Moscow The Beautiful and the Damned*, André Deutsch, 2000. (An English journalist, living in Moscow, records his encounters with ordinary Russians trying to cope with the changes affecting their way of life.)

Robert Service, *A History of Twentieth-century Russia*, Penguin, 1998. (The final chapters cover the period from 1985 to 1997.)

WEBSITES

www. russia.com has news, sections on society and culture and a search facility for further sources of information.

www.sptimes.ru/ has the English-language edition of the twice-weekly *St Petersburg Times*.

www.ru/ is a general information site for news and information about Russia.

GLOSSARY

capitalism   an economic system based on private ownership and the profit motive.

Cold War   state of conflict between the USA and the USSR which emerged after the Second World War and lasted into the late 1980s. Brought to an end by Gorbachev.

communism   To thinkers like Karl Marx, communism is an ideal state where private property is abolished and everyone is equal. The term also describes the political and economic system of the USSR between the 1920s and the late 1980s.

Congress   The Congress of People's Deputies was a parliamentary body established under Gorbachev and replaced by Yeltsin.

coup   a violent or illegal seizure of power.

kapitalizm   Russian for capitalism.

Kremlin   the seat of the Russian government in Moscow.

mafia   a criminal organization, called the mafiya in Russian

NATO (North Atlantic Treaty Organization)   a USA-dominated military alliance set up to oppose the power of the USSR after the Second World War.

oligarchs   the name given to a small number of extremely powerful business people in Russia who influence government policy.

politburo   the central committee of the Communist Party.

privatization   changing a state-owned part of the economy into a privately-owned business.

privitizatsia   Russian for privatization.

Soviet Union   Another name for the USSR.

tsar   the title of the former emperors of Russia.

USSR   the Union of Socialist Soviet Republics, the communist state set up after the revolution in 1917 and disbanded at the end of 1991.

White House   a parliament building in Moscow where elected representatives to the Congress of People's deputies met.

SOURCES

The following were used as sources of information for this book:

Mike Bowker and Cameron Ross (ed.), *Russia After the Cold War*, Longman, 2000

Rose Brady, *Kapitalizm*, Yale University Press, 1999

S. Bridger, R. Kay, K Pinnick, *No More Heroines*, Routledge, 1996

Chrystia Freeland, *Sale of the Century*, Little, Brown and Company, 2000

Carlotta Gall and Thomas De Waal, *Chechnya*, Pan, 1997

Stephen Handleman, *Comrade Criminal*, Yale University Press, 1995

Nick Holdsworth, *Moscow The Beautiful and the Damned*, André Deutsch, 2000

Geoffrey Hoskins and Robert Service (ed.), *Reinterpreting Russia*, Arnold, 1999

Dominic Lieven, *Empire*, John Murray, 2000

Tony Parker, *Russian Voices*, Jonathan Cape, 1991

Hilary Pilkington (ed.), *Gender, Generation and Identity in Contemporary Russia*, Routledge, 1996

David Remnick, *Lenin's Tomb*, Vintage, 1994

Denis J.B. Shaw, *Russia in the Modern World*, Blackwell, 1999

Valerie Sperling, *Organising Women in Contemporary Russia*, Cambridge, 1999

INDEX